POLYAMORY JOURNAL: A RELATIONSHIP BOOK

POLYAMORY JOURNAL

A RELATIONSHIP BOOK

Prompts and Practices for Navigating Non-Monogamy

Kate Kincaid, LPC

ROCKRIDGE
PRESS

Inc. and/or its affiliates in the United States and other countries and may not be used without written permission.

For general information on our other products and services, please contact our Customer Care Department within the United States at (866) 744-2665, or outside the United States at (510) 253-0500.

Paperback ISBN: 978-1-63807-377-2

Manufactured in the United States of America

Interior and Cover Designer: Lindsey Dekker
Art Producer: Samantha Ulban
Editor: Nora Spiegel
Production Editor: Rachel Taenzler
Production Manager: Eric Pier-Hocking

All images used under license iStock. Author photo courtesy of © Rachel Marie Castillo.

10 9 8 7 6 5 4 3 2 1

THIS JOURNAL BELONGS TO

_____

CONTENTS

INTRODUCTION ix

DEFINING YOUR
RELATIONSHIP VALUES 1

FORTIFYING YOUR SELF-SECURITY 29

ESTABLISHING AND
HONORING BOUNDARIES 55

WORKING THROUGH JEALOUSY 81

PRACTICING SELF-CARE 105

THRIVING IN POLYAMORY 131

A FINAL WORD 155

RECOMMENDED RESOURCES 156

REFERENCES 160

INTRODUCTION

This journal is for everyone, no matter how experienced or inexperienced you are with polyamorous relationships. Whether you've just started dreaming about practicing polyamory or you've been ethically non-monogamous for decades, I hope this book becomes a helpful tool for you to better understand yourself and the important people in your life—and to explore and grow into yourself and the life you want.

As a therapist who has worked with hundreds of non-monogamous people in clinical and personal settings, I have gathered a lot of insight into where people get stuck. This journal can help you find your way through the world of non-monogamy as you reflect on what you need and where you want to go.

I've been practicing ethical non-monogamy for about 15 years and what I call unethical non-monogamy for years before that. I didn't know there was a term for my love for multiple people and what I felt was part of my identity. It was only when I took an alternative sexualities class at the Kinsey Institute as an undergraduate that I realized there's a whole world of people like me. This led me to become a licensed therapist who works with queer and ethically non-monogamous people. I'm also a community organizer and the cocreator of Southwest Love Fest, a large festival/ conference on ethical non-monogamy, relationships, identity, and community.

This is not to say that polyamory came easy to me. I have struggled and still do struggle—a lot! But I see it as a healing path aligned with my highest values. I've learned so much about my relational trauma (i.e., the ways I've been harmed in relationships) through my exploration of polyamory, and I add new layers of understanding all the time.

Perhaps you are contemplating opening up your relationship, perhaps you are single and realizing that monogamy hasn't been working for you, or perhaps you're already navigating an open relationship and want to make sure you're doing it in a way that respects yourself and your partner(s). Wherever you are in your journey, I'm glad you're here. It says a lot about you!

A POLYAMORY PRIMER

Before diving into the work, let's get on the same page with language. The word "poly" means "many, several, much," and the word "amor" means "love." So "polyamory" is a term that basically means "many loves." Polyamory falls under the umbrella of ethical non-monogamy (or consensual non-monogamy, a term more commonly used in research settings). There are several other types of relationships under this umbrella, such as swinging, open relationships, relationship anarchy, and others. They all have differences, but they also overlap. This book focuses primarily on polyamory, and I use that term interchangeably with ethical non-monogamy. Feel free to use whatever terms most resonate with you.

Although ethical polyamory is rarely represented in the media, it's more common than you might think. A study published in 2021 found that one in nine Americans have been in a polyamorous relationship and one in six would like to try one. Who is attracted to this lifestyle? Some studies suggest that people interested in polyamory are less neurotic, more extroverted, more open to new experiences, more conscientious, and less sensitive to rejection than the average person. Among millennials, 41 percent reported being interested in an open relationship. This is also true for 29 percent of Gen Zers and 23 percent of Gen Xers. Baby boomers (12 percent) are the least likely to express interest in an open relationship. Self-identified straight people (22 percent) are far less likely than sexual minorities (46 percent)—those who identify as LGBTQIA2S+—to say they are interested in having an open relationship.

These numbers may or may not accurately reflect what's really going on. Things are changing, but many people who identify as polyamorous or some other form of ethically non-monogamous do not feel safe being out about their identity. And there have been and continue to be real consequences for people who do come out. The risk is even higher for people who are multiply marginalized—that is, Queer Trans Black Indigenous People of Color (QTBIPOC). Because of this, QTBIPOC have been underrepresented in research on polyamorous people, despite playing an important role in building our current understanding of polyamory. The practice of non-monogamy goes back millennia and exists across cultures, but polyamory is often seen as a "white people thing." The privileged position of whiteness can protect white polyamorists and allow them to be more out and vocal about their choices.

This is one of many reasons why, when talking about non-monogamy, it's important to reflect on the history of monogamy. In the scope of human evolution, monogamy is actually a relatively new concept. Historically, only about 17 percent of human cultures are strictly monogamous. The vast majority of human societies embrace a mix of relationship types. In his book *Sex at Dawn*, Christopher Ryan posits that, for most of human history, non-monogamy was the norm and that as wealth became concentrated during the Industrial Revolution, monogamy was encouraged as a way to ensure paternity and pass down property.

That may sound like a harsh assessment of monogamy, and I'm not sharing it to be "poly-er than thou" or tell you that everyone should be non-monogamous. Monogamy can be a beautiful and valid choice, especially if it's made consciously and consensually. It's *compulsory* monogamy that can be problematic—and judging by how rampant infidelity is, it seems to be challenging for many people. Whether you're consciously monogamous or not, if going through the prompts and exercises in this journal affirms your monogamous desires, that's great! People who lean toward monogamy can learn a lot from a polyamorous worldview, regardless of what they choose to do in their relationships.

There are many misconceptions about ethical non-monogamy. Perhaps the most common is that it's an excuse for a bunch of sex-crazed people to do whatever they want. That's very far from the case. The vast majority of polyamorous people I've met and worked with care deeply about challenging norms around compulsory monogamy, redefining what relationships can be, and learning to be more authentic and vulnerable. There's a common joke that polyamorists actually have less sex than everyone else because they spend so much time processing their feelings. Research has found that ethically non-monogamous people generally have safer sex practices, talk more openly about sexually transmitted diseases and sexual preferences, and strongly value consent. In other words, sure, the sex can be great, but it's not the primary focus for most polyamorous people.

Ethical versus Unethical Non-Monogamy

You'll notice that I use the terms "ethical non-monogamy" and "consensual non-monogamy," not just "non-monogamy." This is intentional. Being ethical means to live and act within an agreed-upon moral code, and it is a huge part of living this lifestyle. Since this is a marginalized community, much energy has gone into defining its values. Those values include consent, autonomy, flexibility, communality, interdependence, personal responsibility, transformative justice, diversity, acceptance, and inclusivity. (The term "ethical slut" was coined by psychotherapists Dossie Easton and Janet Hardy, and it helped set the tone for the important value of ethical behavior. But I'm going to avoid that one as well because "slut" unfortunately still carries some heavy judgment and doesn't resonate with everyone.)

If a person is a serial cheater, they are practicing non-monogamy, but it's not ethical or consensual for everyone involved. Some common examples of unethical non-monogamy are cheating, coercion, gaslighting, using power and control, and dragging someone along into something they wouldn't necessarily choose. If this sounds like you or someone you love, I hope you (or they) can find the strength and courage to be honest about your desires and be more ethical in your practices. If you have been practicing a form of unethical non-monogamy, I hope this book can help you reveal yourself—someone who is interested in polyamory but struggling with being honest about it—to yourself and others.

Polyamorous Arrangements

The ethical non-monogamy community is not a monolith, and no two polyamorists practice in exactly the same way. Polyamorous relationships can take many forms, and I will mention just a few of them here. People's "polycules" (think of a molecule in chemistry, modeling all the different ways people are connected to their partners and their partners' partners) can be arranged in so many different ways. There are hierarchical and nonhierarchical polyamory, kitchen table or parallel polyamory, solo polyamory, relationship anarchy, and several different structural arrangements such as Vs, quads, triads, and more.

OPEN RELATIONSHIPS

The term "open relationship" is similar to the umbrella term "ethical non-monogamy." Many people use this broader term to define their relationships. These relationships are often more fluid and may describe a variety of practices and beliefs, such as having casual sex and/or being friends with sexual partners but perhaps trying to avoid falling in love. It's best to get clarification on what it means to that particular person or partnership. Swinging is a form of open relationship that usually involves sex with others, often with the partner present and often without romantic or emotional attachments. It can be seen as a way to spice up a relationship without the messiness of emotional connections.

POLYAMORY WITH A HIERARCHY

Hierarchical relationships involve a person giving different priorities and privileges to different partners in some form of hierarchy. Usually there is a primary partner (a life/nesting/anchor partner), a secondary partner, and sometimes other ancillary or tertiary partners. Primary partners usually have the most privilege and are the most prioritized. They often have been together longer, live together, and may share kids and/or finances. Secondary partners usually have less privileges, time, and commitment and are less prioritized. This model is sometimes criticized for labeling someone as secondary without leaving room for the relationship to evolve naturally. Secondaries may feel disregarded and disrespected, and many see this as a vestige of privilege for monogamous couples looking for something more.

RELATIONSHIP ANARCHY

Relationship anarchy is the practice of forming relationships that reject all hierarchies—not just those within romantic relationships. It also rejects the hierarchy that places romantic or sexual relationships above platonic relationships or friendships. In relationship anarchy, there is typically no structure or priorities that people are placed in. Usually that means not saving intimacy or romance just for sexual partners. This model came out of a political ideology as a way to bring anarchist principles to interpersonal relationships.

MONOGAMISH

"Monogamish" is a term coined by author and activist Dan Savage on his podcast Savage Lovecast. It basically means what it sounds like—usually a couple who is mostly monogamous but dabble in ethical non-monogamy from time to time. This often includes rules and agreements about falling in love, dating, and having sex with people while traveling but not maintaining that relationship in their every-day lives.

Another common arrangement is mono/polyam relationships. This is where one (or more) partner is monogamous in practice and one (or more) is polyamorous in practice. The relationship is ethically non-monogamous, but it doesn't require that all people personally identify as polyamorous.

POLYFIDELITOUS

Polyfidelitous, also known as polyexclusivity or polyfi, is a form of polyamory where all members of the group (or polycule) are considered equal partners and agree to be sexually active only with other members. The relationship has more than two people in it, but it is not open to adding more people, at least for the time being. This is sometimes a temporary arrangement that people agree to due to circumstances in their lives, such as having a baby, coping with another stress such as grieving the loss of a family member, or coping with a chronic illness. We saw more of this arrangement in the beginning of the COVID-19 pandemic, when people were trying to reduce their exposure to the virus. Keeping the relationship closed to new partners can help everyone in this non-monogamous arrangement feel secure and know that no one new will be added for the time being. It could also just happen naturally when people didn't plan on being non-monogamous but someone fell in love with another person and it made sense to add them to their lives.

HOW TO USE THIS JOURNAL

Now that we've gone over some basics, let's start figuring out how you can best navigate your own relationship(s). The primary purpose of this journal is to help you get to know yourself better. I believe that everyone has an inner healing intelligence—in other words, you already have all the answers inside yourself, and it's just about connecting to that wisdom. Once you are attuned to yourself and your values, desires, and needs, then you can more authentically share yourself with others.

This book will require challenging, introspective work. I aim to be trauma-informed, which means remembering that trauma (our neurological and emotional responses to terrible events in our history) sometimes overwhelms our nervous system and disconnects us from ourselves and one another. Trauma-informed means to go slowly, stop when you're overwhelmed, and use your resources to work on regulating your physical responses so that you can think more creatively. So nourish yourself as you work on this by drinking water or tea. Wear comfortable clothes. Take breaks, and don't try to do it all in one sitting. Get support by talking to trusted confidants or helping professionals if needed. Personal work and growth are part of a lifelong journey. There's really no rush!

This book is meant to be self-reflective, which means working individually. But we heal in community, so, if possible, please share some of the truths you uncover with the important people in your life—a friend, a partner, or a community discussion circle.

The sections of the book group together themes that are relevant to polyamorous relationships, and each is full of thought-provoking quotes, Q and A sections, journal prompts, and interactive exercises. While this journal is designed to be used from beginning to end, you can also choose your own adventure and simply flip to whichever section is most relevant to you at the time. This is *your* journey, and you can do whatever you want—as long as it's ethical, of course!

It's important to remember that while this journal can be a great supplement to therapy or counseling, it is not a replacement for professional help. There is no shame in seeking professional help in the form of therapy, counseling, coaching, or support groups, and it doesn't mean that you're doing it wrong—quite the opposite, actually. It's hard to see ourselves from the inside out. We need that outside feedback to see ourselves fully.

You can find some helpful information in the Recommended Resources section (page 156) for further reading and therapeutic support. If you are dealing with sexual or emotional abuse or trauma, know that you're not alone and that there is support out there for you.

If You're Interested in Exploring Polyamory . . .

If you are simply curious about polyamory or are just starting to think about opening up your monogamous relationship, use this book as a tool to get to know yourself. It doesn't mean you have to make any changes right now (unless, of course, you want to). You can spend as much time as you like in this self-exploration stage. Try not to think about what all of this will mean and how it will change your relationship; that can come later. I recommend starting with the sections on values and self-care.

If You're Currently in a Polyamorous Relationship . . .

If you are already in a polyamorous relationship, start at the beginning. You may be tempted to jump into the section on what makes polyamorous relationships thrive, but I'll let you in on a little secret: the best relationships I've seen consist of people who are differentiated enough from their partners to be in tune with themselves and what they need as individuals. From that secure base, they can connect intimately with others. So regardless of how experienced you are, use this journal to connect or reconnect with yourself, and watch how that improves all of your relationships.

"VALUES AREN'T BUSES . . .
THEY'RE NOT SUPPOSED TO
GET YOU ANYWHERE.
THEY'RE SUPPOSED TO
DEFINE WHO YOU ARE."

—JENNIFER CRUSIE

DEFINING YOUR RELATIONSHIP VALUES

To be in a healthy relationship, polyamorous or not, it's critical to understand what you truly value in a relationship. Values are the choices you freely make about how you want to act. They are always present and emerge from inside you; they're not hand-me-downs from your parents or your culture, though these factors may influence you. They're not like goals because they're not meant to take you to a specific place or level of achievement. Use this section to get to know what matters most to you, coming from the inside out.

Pretend you have a magic wand. If your relationship(s) could look any way you want, how would it/they look? Focus on the feelings you want, not the form each relationship actually takes.

_____

_____

_____

_____

_____

_____

_____

_____

_____

_____

_____

_____

_____

_____

_____

_____

_____

_____

_____

_____

_____

Values are not goals. They are more like compasses that guide our behavior and let us know we're on the right path and in alignment with our personal values. How do you know when you're in alignment? What does a full-body yes feel like for you?

_____

_____

_____

_____

_____

_____

_____

_____

_____

_____

_____

_____

_____

_____

_____

_____

_____

_____

_____

RANK YOUR PERSONAL VALUES

In this exercise, you will rank some common values to help you think about which ones are important to you personally. Next to each value listed in the table, rate its importance on a scale of 1 to 10, with 1 being not important at all and 10 being extremely important. Then mark how successful you feel you have been at living this value in the past year on a scale of 1 to 10, with 1 being not at all living in accordance with this value and 10 being very aligned. Then, try to rank these values in order of what feels like the highest priority to you right now. If this is challenging and you find yourself reordering a lot, that's totally normal. Try to go with your gut, and don't think too hard about it. You'll find some prompts after the exercise to help you reflect on what came up.

VALUE	IMPORTANCE (1–10)	SUCCESS (1–10)	RANK
Accomplishment			
Adventure			
Aesthetic beauty			
Bravery			
Career			
Community			
Compassion			

VALUE	IMPORTANCE (1–10)	SUCCESS (1–10)	RANK
Connection/relationships			
Creativity			
Dependability			
Education			
Family			
Financial security			
Freedom			
Friendship			
Gratitude			
Leadership			
Learning			
Leisure			
Love			

CONTINUED

CONTINUED

VALUE	IMPORTANCE (1–10)	SUCCESS (1–10)	RANK
Loyalty			
Nature			
Parenting			
Peace			
Physical health			
Romantic/ intimate relationships			
Security			
Self-preservation			
Spirituality			
Success			
Survival			

What are your top three values? What examples in your life show you these values in action?

_____

_____

_____

_____

_____

_____

_____

_____

_____

_____

_____

_____

_____

_____

_____

_____

_____

_____

_____

_____

_____

Which values have you been taught by your family or your culture? Which ones do you want to keep, and which ones can you let go of?

_____

_____

_____

_____

_____

_____

_____

_____

_____

_____

_____

_____

_____

_____

_____

_____

_____

_____

_____

_____

What can you do to become more aligned with the values you've identified here? Are there any life changes you would like to make? What's the first step?

_____

_____

_____

_____

_____

_____

_____

_____

_____

_____

_____

_____

_____

_____

_____

_____

_____

_____

How do I know if something I believe is something I've been taught to believe or something I actually believe?

That's the challenge, isn't it? Usually if a belief is coming from a truth within yourself, it excites and energizes you. You may feel a lightening or uplifting quality in your body. If it's a prescriptive value imposed on you from the outside—one that does not align with your authentic values—it will feel constricting and uncomfortable. You may notice a bit of shame or anger about it because it doesn't fit.

Though it is changing, mononormativity (seeing monogamy as the default and the goal for all romantic relationships) is present in many cultures. What are some of the values that your culture says are important for relationships? Do you agree or disagree? Why?

_____

_____

_____

_____

_____

_____

_____

_____

_____

_____

_____

_____

_____

_____

_____

_____

_____

_____

_____

Connecting with your desires is the first step, one you must complete before you can make any requests for those desires to be fulfilled. Desires can be about anything: Maybe you really want to cut back at work or start the kids in day care, or maybe you've been dreaming of a threesome. What are some of your deepest desires? Don't censor yourself. Let your imagination run wild.

_____

_____

_____

_____

_____

_____

_____

_____

_____

_____

_____

_____

_____

_____

_____

_____

_____

What if my partner and I want
different things?

It's helpful to think about your identity as an individual
before deciding what works for you in relationships.
Often, I see people coming in for relationship therapy
when one person wants to open their relationship and
the other feels like they have no choice. I tell them my
job is to support them both as individuals in deciding what is important and what kinds of relationship
agreements will and won't work for them. The first step,
though, is seeing how you are your own person, separate from but connected to others—even your partner.
You do this by turning inward to figure out your individual values. Then you can find the ways you relate and
overlap as well as the ways in which you may have to
compromise.

RELATIONSHIP RESOURCES

Relationship resources are the ways you show up for other people and how you would like them to show up for you. They tell you what you want from your relationships. The following are common relationship resources for you to rate on a scale of 1 to 10, with 1 being not important and 10 being extremely important. When you've finished, take a moment to really think about your results. Did anything surprise you? Will the results of this exercise cause you to do anything differently in your current relationships?

RELATIONSHIP RESOURCE	IMPORTANCE (1–10)
Affection	
Companionship	
Compatibility	
Emotional intimacy and closeness	
Financial compatibility	
Independence, personal autonomy	
Intellectual rapport and stimulation	
Living together well	
Long-term security and stability	

RELATIONSHIP RESOURCE	IMPORTANCE (1–10)
Privacy	
Quality time	
Romantic love and attention	
Sense of family and community	
Sexual satisfaction	
Shared interests and activities	
Similar values and worldview	
Touch	
Trust and emotional safety	

Imagine doing something that's outside your value system. How does that feel? What do you notice in your body?

_____

_____

_____

_____

_____

_____

_____

_____

_____

_____

_____

_____

_____

_____

_____

_____

_____

_____

_____

_____

Guilt (not to be confused with shame) can let you know you might be doing something that's outside your values. But sometimes it might be someone else's guilt—such as your parents' or an outdated cultural belief—that you've been carrying for too long. How do you know when you are out of alignment with your own chosen values? What are some of the signs you notice?

_____

_____

_____

_____

_____

_____

_____

_____

_____

_____

_____

_____

_____

_____

_____

_____

_____

Sometimes your values become more apparent when you face a crisis. Think about a current or recent stressful situation or crisis you've experienced. In that moment, what do you want to stand for? What can you do and say that you can look back on with no regrets?

_____

_____

_____

_____

_____

_____

_____

_____

_____

_____

_____

_____

_____

_____

_____

_____

_____

_____

_____

"YOUR LIFE IS YOURS TO LIVE,
NO MATTER HOW YOU
CHOOSE TO LIVE IT.
WHEN YOU DO NOT THINK ABOUT
HOW YOU INTEND TO LIVE IT,
IT LIVES YOU.
WHEN YOU OCCUPY IT, STEP INTO
IT CONSCIOUSLY, YOU LIVE IT."

—GARY ZUKAV

Security, love, and safety are universal core human needs. A strategy is the way we think we'll get those needs met (perhaps marriage, monogamy, seat belts). Often, we end up confusing our actual needs with our strategies. For example, we need security and think marriage will provide it. Make a list of your core needs— not the strategies you think will meet those needs.

_____

_____

_____

_____

_____

_____

_____

_____

_____

_____

_____

_____

_____

_____

_____

_____

_____

_____

Sometimes what we want the most is tied to what we fear the most. (For example, we want intimacy, success, connection, but we fear vulnerability, failure, not being enough, isolation.) What are some of your fears? What desires do they point to? Write down a few fears and then think about a potential related desire for each one.

_____

_____

_____

_____

_____

_____

_____

_____

_____

_____

_____

_____

_____

_____

_____

_____

_____

One way to get more clarity about your values is to think about what's important to you and what legacy you want to leave behind. Imagine being a fly on the wall at your funeral while your loved ones are all sharing about your life. What do you hope they will be saying about you? How would you have liked to contribute to the world or shaped other people's lives?

_____

_____

_____

_____

_____

_____

_____

_____

_____

_____

_____

_____

_____

_____

_____

_____

_____

What qualities do you value in a partner? A friend?

_____

_____

_____

_____

_____

_____

_____

_____

_____

_____

_____

_____

_____

_____

_____

_____

_____

_____

_____

_____

Identify six people who are important role models for you. Think of the values they embody and write them down. For example, your list might include "my grandmother for her warmth, openness, and unconditional love."

_____

_____

_____

_____

_____

_____

_____

_____

_____

_____

_____

_____

_____

_____

_____

_____

_____

_____

_____

ALIGNING WITH YOUR VALUES

Another way to better understand when you are in alignment with your values is to work backward and think about how you feel in various everyday situations. When you feel the most like yourself, this is likely when you are in alignment with your personal values. When you feel incongruent or out of place, this might indicate that you're acting in ways that don't line up with the values that are important to you.

Think about situations where you feel the most authentic or out of place, and fill out the table below.

	WHEN I FEEL AUTHENTIC	WHEN I FEEL OUT OF PLACE
Who I'm with		
What I'm doing		
Feelings or thoughts that come up		
How I feel afterward		

MAKE A COMMITMENT TO YOUR VALUES

Now let's dig a little deeper with one value that you want to commit to further integrating into your life. It can be anything, but perhaps try to think of something related to your interest in practicing polyamory. Choose one value from one of your previous lists or a different one you've thought of and use it to work through the following questions. You can do this exercise with other important values, too.

What is the value you'd like to see more of in your life?

_____

_____

What is a goal related to this value that you'd like to accomplish?

_____

_____

_____

What is one or more smaller action steps you feel will take you closer to achieving the goal?

_____

_____

What personal challenges might these committed action steps cause to arise? Think about any physical and psychological feelings, unproductive/unpleasant self-criticisms, thoughts, or memories. How can you overcome them?

_____

_____

_____

"TO LOVE ONESELF

IS THE BEGINNING OF

A LIFELONG ROMANCE."

—OSCAR WILDE

FORTIFYING YOUR SELF-SECURITY

It's normal to have feelings of self-doubt and low self-esteem from time to time. This is especially true when your relationships don't feel secure. And opening up your relationships makes them inherently more unstable and less secure, at least temporarily. But the feeling of self-security is something that can be intentionally cultivated and maintained despite your circumstances. It is possible to work on a secure attachment with yourself regardless of what is going on with your relationships. The more you trust, accept, and have compassion for yourself, the easier all of your relationships will be, polyamorous or otherwise.

What do you love most about yourself?

_____

_____

_____

_____

_____

_____

_____

_____

_____

_____

_____

_____

_____

_____

_____

_____

_____

_____

_____

_____

_____

What do other people love about you?

_____

_____

_____

_____

_____

_____

_____

_____

_____

_____

_____

_____

_____

_____

_____

_____

_____

_____

_____

_____

Think about all the amazing things you have to offer. Just for fun, even if you're not looking to date, write your online dating profile. What's lovable about you?

_____

_____

_____

_____

_____

_____

_____

_____

_____

_____

_____

_____

_____

_____

_____

_____

_____

_____

_____

_____

Think about your signals when you're feeling insecure. What does your body do? What thoughts arise? How do you normally work through these feelings?

_____

_____

_____

_____

_____

_____

_____

_____

_____

_____

_____

_____

_____

_____

_____

_____

_____

_____

_____

I often tell my clients that going "one up" (everyone sucks) or "one down" (everyone is cooler than me)—no matter the direction—usually indicates a dip in self-worth. Do you find yourself doing this? If so, in what ways?

_____

_____

_____

_____

_____

_____

_____

_____

_____

_____

_____

_____

_____

_____

_____

_____

_____

_____

_____

_____

Think of a time when you were in the presence of someone who was confident and unapologetic about who they are. How did it make you feel? What did you notice about them?

_____

_____

_____

_____

_____

_____

_____

_____

_____

_____

_____

_____

_____

_____

_____

_____

_____

TUNE IN TO YOUR HIGHEST SELF

Eye movement desensitization and reprocessing (EMDR) is an effective psycho-therapeutic treatment for trauma. One of the last steps in EMDR is a practice of connecting to an embodied sense of your highest self. That's the self that is always there but is often hidden by parts of your personality that are trying to protect you from being vulnerable—and that may unintentionally hinder authentic connection. You can find EMDR playlists on YouTube or Spotify that feature instrumental music that stimulates both hemispheres of the brain. Or you can do the butterfly hug. Basically, you cross your arms in front of you to hug yourself and then tap each hand on the opposite upper arm or shoulder, one hand at a time. This will activate bilateral stimulation—repeatedly stimulating one side of the brain and then the other—which is one of the keys that make EMDR work. Close your eyes, listen to the playlist, or do the butterfly hug while you envision your best self.

- Imagine what you look like when you feel confident, free, expansive, and loving.

- Imagine how it would feel in your body to feel this way.

- Imagine how others would react to you if you embodied this feeling while interacting with them.

What was that like? What did you notice in your body?

_____

_____

_____

_____

_____

_____

How would your life be different if you were more deeply rooted in your own self-worth? How would knowing that you have inherent value, no matter the external circumstances, change how you approach daily stressors and conflicts with people?

_____

_____

_____

_____

_____

_____

_____

_____

_____

_____

_____

_____

_____

_____

_____

_____

_____

_____

_____

FINDING YOUR YES

Trusting yourself is key to creating more self-security. Saying yes to what you want and no to what you don't want helps you build trust within yourself. Think of something that you have to decide whether to say yes or no to. Some examples might be a social invitation, a request from a colleague at work, a favor from a family member, or a request related to polyamory from your partner(s). Use the questions in this exercise to check in with yourself before saying yes. If the answers to these questions are not "yes," it might mean your answer to this situation is "no" or "maybe" or "not right now."

- Have I had enough time to really evaluate this decision? If not, can I ask for more time?

- Do I have enough information to assess this situation and how it may affect me? If not, what else do I need to know?

- Can I really say no or maybe? Do I have any meaningful alternatives or options that will work better for me?

How was this exercise valuable in helping you tune in to how you want to respond to requests from people in your life?

_____

_____

_____

_____

_____

_____

_____

When threatened, everyone tends toward one or more of these self-protective reactions: fight, flight, freeze, or fawn. You've probably heard of fight or flight, but sometimes you might feel frozen or stuck when your nervous system is overwhelmed. Or you might fawn, which means to flatter or be overly nice and likable when you're feeling scared or threatened. Think about your own nervous system tendencies. Start by paying attention to how your body and mind respond to stressful situations. What do you tend to do? How do different stressors bring out different responses?

_____

_____

_____

_____

_____

_____

_____

_____

_____

_____

_____

_____

_____

_____

_____

_____

Staying steady in the face of stressful situations and consciously moving through your habitual fight, flight, freeze, or fawn reactions is a skill that can be taught, practiced, and maintained. No one is born with this ability. The more you do it, the easier it gets. List all the reasons it would benefit you, other people, and your relationships to learn to stay steadier.

_____

_____

_____

_____

_____

_____

_____

_____

_____

_____

_____

_____

_____

_____

_____

_____

I usually feel sure of myself in my work and as a friend, but when it comes to polyamory, I seem to turn into a teenager, and I often feel so insecure. How do I handle that?

First of all, this is normal! Relationship stress can cause anyone to regress, especially if you have unresolved interpersonal trauma. That's why, as a relationship therapist, I basically use the same skills with adults that I would use with children. I don't do this to be condescending but rather to address the reality that when we are triggered, our higher-order, adult-thinking brain temporarily goes offline. With practice, we can learn to reparent ourselves and tend to this young part of ourselves. And once we do that, we can grow ourselves back up and relate to our partners from our most mature selves.

It's not uncommon to feel vulnerable and insecure as you start out exploring polyamory. None of us are comfortable in the face of rejection, jealousy, or feeling inadequate, and these are common triggers for even the bravest, most secure polyamorists. Grounding techniques are essential tools to use when your nervous system is over- or underactivated. They can be used to help get you out of your head and into the present moment, which is usually less scary than the past or the future that's replaying in your head. Some examples of grounding techniques are clenching and releasing your fists, noticing how your feet feel on the floor, noticing five pink things in the room, and snapping a rubber band on your wrist. What helps you feel more grounded and present in the room?

_____

_____

_____

_____

_____

_____

_____

_____

_____

_____

_____

_____

_____

KEEP A LIST OF AFFIRMATIONS

Affirmations are simple phrases that affirm who you are and something about the world. They are powerful because, when you repeat them, they can help strengthen beliefs that you have or want to have. When you make an affirmation, it should be in the present tense—as if it is already true, not something you want or are working toward. For example, a good affirmation might be: "I am kind and loving and loved." Write down a few affirmations. Then write them on multiple sticky notes and post them on your bathroom mirror or refrigerator. When you see a note, say the affirmation to yourself. Or maybe you want to schedule affirmations as a weekly text you receive on your phone, reminding you of how amazing you are. Or simply tab this page and review your affirmations periodically when you need a pick-me-up.

When you're feeling particularly triggered or reactive, whether that's because of the fear of your partner starting to date someone else, the pain of rejection, or the changes in your relationship, it's helpful to focus on the fundamentals, such as food, sleep, and physical comfort. What's a basic need you often forget? How can you give it to yourself?

_____

_____

_____

_____

_____

_____

_____

_____

_____

_____

_____

_____

_____

_____

_____

_____

_____

_____

There's a saying I often use with clients: "Don't shoot the second arrow." The first arrow is the painful or scary situation that you are facing; the second arrow is your reactions that try to deflect discomfort in response to that situation, such as making excuses, blaming, or self-criticism. You often don't have control of the first arrow, but you definitely can control the second one. How do you treat yourself when you make a mistake or are struggling with something? How can you gently catch yourself and be kinder to yourself as you struggle?

Think of three unhelpful beliefs about yourself that you're ready to release. Write them here. Or write them on a piece of paper and burn it.

_____

_____

_____

_____

_____

_____

_____

_____

_____

_____

_____

_____

_____

_____

_____

_____

_____

_____

EMBODYING CONFIDENCE

How you position and carry your body can greatly affect your mood and your emotions. Let's try a little exercise to feel this effect. Stand or sit where you can see yourself in a mirror. Hunch your shoulders and arrange your face as it might look when you are feeling scared or alone or insecure.

Now consciously shift your body into a more confident position. Roll your shoulders back, stand or sit up tall, and hold your head high. Maybe even stretch your arms out and take up more space than usual. Allow a confident, knowing smile to come across your lips. Look yourself square in the eye. What differences did you notice in how you feel inside? Notice how powerful body movements and positioning are in creating your reality.

_____

_____

_____

_____

_____

_____

_____

_____

_____

_____

_____

_____

_____

"KNOWING OTHERS IS INTELLIGENCE; KNOWING YOURSELF IS TRUE WISDOM. MASTERING OTHERS IS STRENGTH; MASTERING YOURSELF IS TRUE POWER."

—LAO TZU

A lot of what I read tells me it's my job to become more secure and that I should "take responsibility for my feelings." How do I do that better?

You're right. A lot of the popular polyamory advice does advocate for this, and I see the intent, but I think this commonly given advice is lacking something. Of course, it's good to look at yourself and take responsibility for your thoughts, feelings, and actions. However, we are interdependent beings; we affect one another in powerful ways. If the environment is supportive, we see that people are more resilient and better able to handle difficult emotions like jealousy and insecurity. So, yes, it's important to "own your stuff," but that's only part of the picture. We also need to create communities and polycules that support us wherever we are in our journey of self-security.

Our communities can be a great source of support and security. Who in your community can help you remember what's great about you when you're having trouble remembering it?

_____

_____

_____

_____

_____

_____

_____

_____

_____

_____

_____

_____

_____

_____

_____

_____

_____

_____

Attachment is a survival need that drives us to seek closeness and feel safe. There are different attachment styles, including secure attachment and four types of insecure attachment: anxious preoccupied, anxious avoidant, fearful avoidant, and disorganized attachment, which is a mix of the other three insecure styles. Attachment styles are not inherent to one's character—you can be attached in different ways in different relationships. They are also not fixed or permanent; they can be healed and repatterned. What do you notice about your tendencies in close relationships? Do you have different patterns with different people, or have you noticed a common trend across all of your relationships? Try not to diagnose or judge yourself; just notice if there are any tendencies.

Aloneness is being with the presence of yourself, which differs from being lonely. It's not something many of us are practiced in—that is, being present with ourselves and enjoying it. How do you feel just being alone with yourself? Think about the last time you were alone for an extended period of time. What was it like? What was hard about it? What did you enjoy about it?

_____

_____

_____

_____

_____

_____

_____

_____

_____

_____

_____

_____

_____

_____

_____

_____

ENVISION SELF-SECURITY

Vision boards are amazing ways to explore your feelings without words and engage different parts of your brain. Gather up some old magazines or catalogs that you're done with. If you don't have any, you can usually find these at places like used bookstores and doctor's offices. Put on some good music, and without thinking too hard about it, cut out words or images that represent self-confidence and self-security to you. Arrange them on a piece of paper and tape or glue them down. The final product should inspire you to bring more of these qualities into your life. Hang it somewhere you will see it often.

"YOUR TASK IS NOT TO SEEK FOR LOVE, BUT MERELY TO SEEK AND FIND ALL THE BARRIERS WITHIN YOURSELF THAT YOU HAVE BUILT AGAINST IT."

—HELEN SCHUCMAN

ESTABLISHING AND HONORING BOUNDARIES

O ur relationships are built and maintained on a set of common agreements—*boundaries* of acceptable conduct. Boundaries help us know where our responsibility starts and ends. Establishing relationship boundaries is a critical step for anyone considering or entering into a polyamorous relationship because they can help us maintain safety and connection to ourselves and our partners. This might feel awkward or formal at first if you're not used to it, but setting healthy boundaries actually helps us feel closer and more intimate with our friends, family, and lovers. Respectfully navigating those boundaries, communicating about agreements, and allowing them to evolve and change are equally important.

You navigate agreements about boundaries with not just your lovers but also your friends, boss/employee, everyone in your book club, kid(s), neighbors, restaurant server, and housemate(s). Think of one of these people and identify a few agreements you have made or could make with them.

_____

_____

_____

_____

_____

_____

_____

_____

_____

_____

_____

_____

_____

_____

_____

_____

_____

_____

_____

_____

_____

Agreements require the active participation of at least two people. Agreements also require that both parties:

- Understand the agreement

- Understand any consequences for breaking it

- Have the freedom to say yes or no (otherwise it's a demand)

Can you think of a time when you were being asked to enter into an agreement when one of these three aspects was missing? How was that for you?

_____

_____

_____

_____

_____

_____

_____

_____

_____

_____

_____

_____

_____

_____

We often communicate with a goal in mind—to connect, ask for support or comfort, relay information, make a decision, or solve a problem (to name just a few). Think about how you communicate when you just want to connect. What words and gestures do you use to let someone know what you are looking for? How is that communication different from when you are trying to solve a problem or receive comfort or support?

_____

_____

_____

_____

_____

_____

_____

_____

_____

_____

_____

_____

_____

_____

_____

_____

_____

Emotional honesty is a common core value in ethically non-monogamous communities. The first step in being emotionally honest is to be honest with yourself about what you are feeling. And the next step is to bravely communicate it to someone else in a clear way. Can you think of anything that you might need to admit to yourself—and eventually another person? It's okay if you haven't been able to do it yet; this is really hard!

_____

_____

_____

_____

_____

_____

_____

_____

_____

_____

_____

_____

_____

_____

_____

_____

_____

A CONVERSATION SET AND SETTING

"Set and setting" is a phrase used in the psychedelic world to describe the importance of both environment and mindset in creating a comfortable experience for vulnerability and exploration. Think of an important conversation you want to have. Perhaps you have a request you want to make in your relationship, or you want to discuss a time when you felt a boundary was crossed. Take some time to make the physical environment conducive to connection. Turn off the TV, silence your phone, light a candle, wear something comfortable. Now, take a moment to explore your mindset and reflect on the following questions.

What are your goals for this conversation?

_____

_____

What do you feel in your body as you prepare for this conversation?

_____

_____

What are the important personal points to get across?

_____

_____

How do you want to be seen and heard?

_____

_____

When you've completed this exercise, reflect on how taking the time to address set and setting affected the conversation you wanted to have.

There are four basic communication styles: assertive, aggressive, passive, and passive-aggressive. They may show up differently depending on the relationship. For example, if you are a supervisor at your job, you might feel more comfortable being assertive and making clear requests of your supervisees, but you may still struggle to ask for what you need in your romantic relationships and end up communicating in a more passive or passive-aggressive way. What do you think are your communication style(s)? In which relationships do you find it harder to be assertive? Why?

_____

_____

_____

_____

_____

_____

_____

_____

_____

_____

_____

_____

_____

_____

_____

_____

THE ART OF ASKING

Making clear requests is important for maintaining healthy boundaries in relationships because they help you unambiguously notify your partner when you need something. Often people think they've clearly asked for something, but it wasn't clear to their partner(s). There are ways to make it more likely that you will be heard and understood by not only your partner(s) but also everyone in your life.

1. Write down your request. Just let it come out naturally.

    _____

    _____

2. Then write the request more like a demand, as if you're telling the other person that this is what is required and this is what's happening.

    _____

    _____

3. Then ask in a more vulnerable way—a way that reveals a deep desire or need of yours.

    _____

    _____

4. Now write out what you're afraid might happen if you make this request.

    _____

    _____

5. Remind yourself that you're asking this to share a desire, to be seen or known, not necessarily to get what you want. Now write your request again.

    _____

    _____

Write a short letter to your current or future lover about what you need to feel safe and secure. Here you can share some of your known physical, emotional, and sexual boundaries.

_____

_____

_____

_____

_____

_____

_____

_____

_____

_____

_____

_____

_____

_____

_____

_____

_____

_____

_____

_____

How do you know what other people's physical, emotional, and sexual boundaries are? Think about nonverbal signals, too.

_____

_____

_____

_____

_____

_____

_____

_____

_____

_____

_____

_____

_____

_____

_____

_____

_____

_____

_____

A lot of people are unclear on what constitutes a boundary violation. They might know the obvious ones, like physical abuse or sexual assault, but not realize that it's also not okay for someone to yell at you, look in your phone without your permission, or demand you talk about something when you've said you don't want to right now. These are, in fact, real boundary violations. What are your boundary violations? Describe them below.

_____

_____

_____

_____

_____

_____

_____

_____

_____

_____

_____

_____

_____

_____

_____

_____

_____

Boundaries are about you and your own actions; they are not about what other people can and can't do. For example, you might say, "I won't have unprotected sex with you if you have unprotected sex with others" and act accordingly. But telling someone else that they can't have the kind of sex they want to with others would violate that person's bodily autonomy. What are your boundaries when it comes to sexual practices?

_____

_____

_____

_____

_____

_____

_____

_____

_____

_____

_____

_____

_____

_____

_____

"LOVE RECOGNIZES NO BARRIERS."

—MAYA ANGELOU

What if I didn't know something crossed my boundaries until after the fact?

You can spend a lot of time thinking about all the hypothetical situations and making agreements based on how you think you're going to feel. But often it's not until you start practicing polyamory that you run into boundaries that you didn't even know you had. That's why it's important to be continuously checking in with your partners about your changing needs and desires. With practice and experience, you'll be more aware of your boundaries and can assert them more clearly.

We often talk about consent in the context of sexual encounters, but the concept runs much deeper within our relationships; it's ultimately about respecting one another's autonomy. There are four tenets of consent: consent must be clear, coherent, willing, and ongoing. How can you make your current relationships more consensual? Can you think of something that happened recently, in any area of your life, where you practiced good consent?

_____

_____

_____

_____

_____

_____

_____

_____

_____

_____

_____

_____

_____

_____

_____

_____

_____

Boundaries are a two-way street: they protect us from others and contain us so that we can protect others from ourselves. When we protect ourselves, we are showing self-respect or self-love by tending to our own needs. When we contain ourselves, we are being respectful of others and their needs. Issues about boundaries arise when we start protecting and containing ourselves too much (such as shutting down and not being able to listen to a partner sharing vulnerable feelings) or too little (for example, sharing our whole trauma history with a person when we haven't yet determined their ability to safely hold that information). In what ways do you struggle with protection and/or containment?

LISTENER ROLES, SPEAKER ROLES

One of the most challenging ways boundary issues show up is in communication. That's why, when I do relationship therapy, we spend a lot of time talking about communication dynamics and practicing communicating about less triggering topics. Think of a mild frustration you could talk to a friend or partner about; then practice being the speaker and practice being the listener. Before we do this in my office, I give my clients a list of responsibilities for each role so that everyone knows what their role entails. Find another person to practice with in one role and then switch to the other.

Speaker Responsibilities: To Reveal Oneself

- Focus on one issue at a time.

- Check your listener's readiness.

- Describe what you want.

- Share how you feel right now; then share what's underneath the initial feeling.

- Allow yourself to be vulnerable about your feelings so that your listener can get to know the real you.

- Remind yourself that you have a role to play in being understood.

Listener Responsibilities: To Understand Another

- Listen calmly. Don't defend yourself, argue, or complain.

- Ask yourself: "Am I in a place to listen with openness?"

- Ask questions. Develop an interested and curious state of mind.

- Remember that it's your responsibility to manage your reactions.

- Repeat back to your partner what you understand.

- Remind yourself to just listen and not look for solutions yet.

Hopefully, this exercise helped you better understand the different responsibilities associated with being the speaker and the listener. What was this exercise like for you? Did you find it easier to be in one role over the other?

The idea of being vulnerable seems to be increasingly valued, especially in communities where people are trying to relate more authentically. But vulnerability can mean different things to different people. What does being vulnerable mean to you? What feelings does the word "vulnerability" bring up in you? What situations make you feel vulnerable?

_____

_____

_____

_____

_____

_____

_____

_____

_____

_____

_____

_____

_____

_____

_____

_____

_____

Disclosure—that is, how much you share with another person about your other romantic/sexual relationships—is something that has to be negotiated when you're practicing polyamory. Some people want to know everything, and others don't want to know anything. Neither way is better; it all depends on you and your partner(s)' preferences. How much disclosure do you think you want from your partners? How much do you like to share?

_____

_____

_____

_____

_____

_____

_____

_____

_____

_____

_____

_____

_____

_____

_____

_____

_____

Every time I see movies about people in ethically non-monogamous relationships, I feel like I desire that kind of relationship, but I wonder if I can do it in real life. How do I know whether this is something I actually want to do?

First of all, you should know this is a very common experience. Our ideals and desires don't always align with our reality, so it's great that you're asking yourself this. There's no one right way to do polyamory. What matters is knowing and asserting what you need to make your relationships work for you. It's important that you spend some time clarifying your relationship values, basic needs and wants, and boundaries in any relationship. There are many great exercises in this book to help you do that. Remember that just because something is hard or scary doesn't mean it's not for you. And just because you desire something doesn't mean it's what's best for you at this time in your life. Either way, the place to start is to focus on yourself.

Newly polyamorous people often want to have a lot of rules. This is an attempt to increase safety, but it can also be really stifling and, paradoxically, often leaves people feeling more insecure. This is normal! Often the rules and agreements evolve and become less rigid as people get more comfortable and experienced and as trust is built. Write out all of your rules. Which should you keep? Which can you let go of or simplify? Think of areas that are hard no's and areas where you can be more flexible.

There are often several possible approaches to getting your most important relationship needs met. For example, perhaps physical connection is a strong need of yours, and the ways you can feel that need is met in a relationship are tickles while watching TV, foot rubs after a long day, hugs before you go to work, and a regular date to open up to connecting sexually. Write down a few needs and then think of all the ways you can get each of those needs met. Keep in mind, though, that it's not mandatory that you have many different possibilities for meeting every need. It's okay to just have one or two.

_____

_____

_____

_____

_____

_____

_____

_____

_____

_____

_____

_____

_____

_____

_____

GET COMFORTABLE WITH NO

Most people don't like to hear the word "no." It can remind of us being scolded as a child. But no is an opportunity for you to know where someone's boundaries are, and knowing that helps create trust. It takes practice to get comfortable with hearing no and not spinning out into a shame or blame spiral. If you've ever been to a cuddle or play party, one of the exercises is to practice saying no. People pair up, say no to whatever the other person asks and then switch roles. It's an amazingly powerful exercise because most people do feel activated by hearing no, even if it's to something they were just pretending to want or would never even want! This exercise requires another person, so find a trusted friend or partner and have them say no to anything you ask. You could take it one step further and find multiple people to practice with. It's also good to practice being the one who says no, as this can also bring up a lot of feelings. It's hard to deny people what they want, but with good practice it gets easier and easier to maintain your boundaries despite what others may want.

Think of a time when an important boundary of yours was crossed. How do you know when a boundary has been crossed? What body sensations do you notice immediately and as you think back on it? What do you tend to do in these situations? What do you wish you had done differently? Now flip the perspective. Has there been a time when you crossed a boundary or broke an agreement in your relationship? How did you handle it?

_____

_____

_____

_____

_____

_____

_____

_____

_____

_____

_____

_____

_____

_____

_____

_____

_____

FIND YOUR YES/NO/MAYBE

Yes/No/Maybe lists are popular in the polyamory and the kink/BDSM world. They can be a really fun way to explore what you and your partner(s) want and where your boundaries are. You can find many Yes/No/Maybe lists online, or you can make your own right here.

Here are some ideas to get you started.

- Spanking a partner for sexual pleasure **Yes | No | Maybe**

- Sex with two partners at a time **Yes | No | Maybe**

- Casual or occasional open sexual relationships **Yes | No | Maybe**

- Serious or ongoing open romantic relationships **Yes | No | Maybe**

ACTIVITY/RELATIONSHIP FACTOR	YES	NO	MAYBE

"JEALOUSY IS ALL THE FUN
YOU THINK THEY HAD."

—ERICA JONG

WORKING THROUGH JEALOUSY

Jealousy is one of the most frequent and significant challenges faced by people in polyamorous relationships. When jealousy comes up, it does not mean you're an insecure person or that you can't be polyamorous. It's a normal emotion that everyone feels regardless of their relationship orientation. And while you can't avoid feeling jealous from time to time, you can change how you respond to it. Recognizing and working through jealousy—both your own and your partner's—is a skill. Like any skill, it can be learned, practiced, and mastered. Polyamorous people aren't necessarily less jealous than monogamous people—they're just bravely learning to tolerate and cope with this emotion.

Let's jump right in and do a free write about jealousy. Anything is okay! Think about your history with jealousy and what messages you've gotten about what jealousy is and why it arises.

_____

_____

_____

_____

_____

_____

_____

_____

_____

_____

_____

_____

_____

_____

_____

_____

_____

_____

_____

_____

What are your strongest jealousy triggers?

_____

_____

_____

_____

_____

_____

_____

_____

_____

_____

_____

_____

_____

_____

_____

_____

_____

_____

_____

Physiologically, jealousy often feels very similar to excitement and passion but with more fear and anger mixed in. What does jealousy feel like in your body? What happens to your face, hands, chest, and stomach when you feel jealous? What other emotions feel like that, too?

_____

_____

_____

_____

_____

_____

_____

_____

_____

_____

_____

_____

_____

_____

_____

_____

_____

_____

_____

HELPFUL VS. UNHELPFUL JEALOUSY

It's not always easy to differentiate between helpful jealousy (something that poses a real threat to the viability of your relationship) and unhelpful jealousy (something that is rooted in fear and your own beliefs about yourself). Here are some hallmarks of helpful jealousy.

- You have something that you fear losing. (Remember, a perceived loss can create as strong a reaction as an actual loss!)

- You perceive that someone else wants the same thing (which is very easy to do because we often project our own desires onto other people).

- You believe there's a scarcity of that resource. (Usually there is not a scarcity of love, but there might be a real scarcity of time.)

- You believe you'd lose in a competition. (This is a tricky one because you'd have to trust your partner not to make it a competition between two people.)

Unless *all four* are present, your jealousy is likely an unhelpful distortion of the situation. I don't want to minimize real threats to your relationship(s), and as I've said before, polyamory can be risky and destabilizing. But unhelpful jealousy (i.e., jealousy rooted in fear) is the more common feeling. I hope this comes as a relief, but this type of jealousy can feel just as real as an actual threat, so be gentle with yourself if you're having big emotions. Almost everyone has felt jealousy from time to time. If you are experiencing unhelpful jealousy, what do you need? What reassurances could help you? What does reassurance look like for you?

_____

_____

_____

_____

_____

PLAY OUT THE WORST-CASE SCENARIO

This may be a little counterintuitive, but sometimes letting ourselves think all the way through to the worst-case scenario reveals how unlikely it is—or how we would still survive. In your mind, play the tape forward of your worst fear coming true. How would you learn to be okay? This exercise may require some practice at nervous system regulation, so don't push yourself too hard. Try some deep belly breathing (or any other grounding technique you know works for you) before, during, and after this exercise. Remind yourself that this is a hypothetical exercise, and though it might feel real to your body, it is not what is really happening. You might want to do this with a trusted coach, mentor, or therapist if you have one. Shake it out or dance ecstatically afterward to discharge the feelings that came up.

We all have a window of tolerance; how big it is depends on how activated our nervous system is in any situation. Sometimes we're too shut down to engage. Sometimes we're too activated and aren't thinking clearly. In moments like these, ask for a slowdown—not saying no to something but rather saying, "Whoa, I need to calm down." How do you know when you're beyond your window of tolerance? Do you tend to be under- or overactivated?

When feelings of jealousy come up, we often look to the people in our romantic relationships to help us work through them. But leaning on trusted friends can sometimes feel more supportive and less charged. Identify three friends with whom you can talk openly about your feelings of jealousy.

_____

_____

_____

_____

_____

_____

_____

_____

_____

_____

_____

_____

_____

_____

_____

_____

_____

_____

"LOVE FLOWERS BEST IN OPENNESS AND FREEDOM."

—EDWARD ABBEY

CIRCLES OF SUPPORT

It's important to remember to connect and rely on supports outside your relationship. So often in our mononormative culture, people form a community of two—themselves and their one partner. Polyamory is a beautiful way to extend that community. But let's take it even further beyond whomever you're romantically or sexually involved with. Use the graphic on the following page to identify your circles of support. This activity can help you identify all of the supports around you.

First, think of whom you are closest to, your primary support people, those you are most intimate with. This could be your romantic partner(s) or a platonic life partner. Write their names in the center ring. Then in the next ring (close community), identify friends and other people you may regularly see but who wouldn't be the first people you'd go to when you need something. The next ring out (extended community) would be colleagues, neighbors, coworkers—people you may see often but with whom you don't share intimate details about your life. The last ring is for acquaintances. Perhaps these are people you'd like to bring closer into the middle of the circle, but it takes time to build those relationships. Or perhaps these are people who for whatever reason are more on the periphery of your life, although they may have specific roles for how they might help or support you.

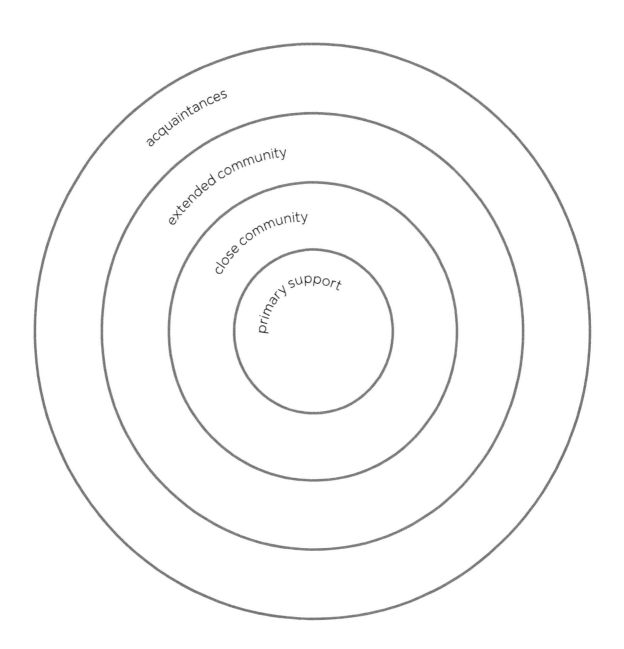

acquaintances

extended community

close community

primary support

We all have wounded parts of ourselves that are not fully grown up. Internal Family Systems, a psychotherapeutic theory, suggests that these are younger "exiled" parts that our older "protector" parts try to manage. Jealousy often arises from a protector part; it's trying to make sure you're protected from getting hurt. Instead of denying your jealousy, try giving it more attention. Paradoxically, this often eases the underlying emotions and helps you feel more in control. Give the pen to your jealous part; what does that part of you want to say? Don't censor it or judge it; just let the words flow.

_____

_____

_____

_____

_____

_____

_____

_____

_____

_____

_____

_____

_____

_____

_____

Think of the moments when you did something out of jealousy that you would like to forgive yourself for. Write them down. Then try to give yourself some compassion and forgiveness. Remember that we're always trying our best with the tools we have.

_____

_____

_____

_____

_____

_____

_____

_____

_____

_____

_____

_____

_____

_____

_____

_____

_____

_____

_____

FINDING THE RAW SPOTS

Often jealousy covers up more primary emotions such as fear, panic, or pain. It's important to look at what's below the jealousy. Look at the following words and circle the ones that feel true for you deep down in moments when you are disconnected.

Ashamed	Hurt	Panicked
Broken	Inadequate	Rejected
Confused	Insignificant	Sad
Disappointed	Intimidated	Scared
Dismissed	Isolated	Unimportant
Disposable	Lonely	Unsafe
Helpless	Lost	Unwanted
Hopeless	Misunderstood	Vulnerable
Humiliated	Overwhelmed	Worried

Do you show these feelings to your partner(s)? If not, what do you usually show them? For example, often we show anger when we feel scared or unsafe. In this case, the anger would be the secondary emotion, which is covering up the primary emotion of fear or vulnerability.

_____

_____

_____

_____

_____

Shame attacks happen when we feel bad about who we are and how we've acted. Often this comes after feeling jealous and acting out. We feel ashamed of the jealousy, so we try to protect ourselves by turning our attention outward and blaming others (our partners, our partners' other partners . . .). What happens when you're feeling ashamed? In what ways do you try to blame others for your discomfort? What are the consequences of this?

_____

_____

_____

_____

_____

_____

_____

_____

_____

_____

_____

_____

_____

_____

_____

_____

_____

_____

My partner has a few partners, and I feel supportive of those relationships. When it comes to me dating, though, my partner is really insecure and is constantly making oppressive rules about my behavior. It feels like a double standard. What should I do?

Dating/loving multiple people and being comfortable with our partners dating/loving multiple people are two separate skills. It sounds like your partner needs some help with the latter skill. It's important to understand that different people have different tendencies and needs. While you may have an easier time working through jealousy, your partner struggles with it. It doesn't mean they get to set your boundaries. Remember, boundaries explain what you will and won't stand for, not what others can and can't do. If dating others is important to you, it's important to assert that and negotiate what agreements feel good for both of you, not just your partner. At the same time, your partner needs to work on strengthening the skill of tolerating jealousy and not controlling your behavior.

Working through jealousy means trusting others to act in a way that is honorable to themselves and to your relationship(s). It's hard to do that when you're feeling afraid and insecure. What are all the ways you can trust your significant other(s)? Even if it's just that they always remember to pick up dog food when it's running low, this demonstrates attentiveness. If more trust needs to be built, what would that look like?

_____

_____

_____

_____

_____

_____

_____

_____

_____

_____

_____

_____

_____

_____

_____

_____

_____

I often tell my newly polyamorous clients that jealousy is data. It can show you what you desire. What might your jealousies be showing you that you want? For example, if you felt very jealous because your partner took their new partner to a fancy restaurant downtown, perhaps you'd like to do something similar. You can learn to ask for what you want rather than be hurt by what you're not getting. What do you want that you haven't asked for?

Jealousy makes you very vulnerable. It can actually bring you closer to your partner(s) if you share it in a way that speaks your truth, what you desire, and what you need—and if your lover(s) can be in a place to hear and see that truth. Can you think of any times when sharing your jealousy actually made you feel closer in a relationship?

_____

_____

_____

_____

_____

_____

_____

_____

_____

_____

_____

_____

_____

_____

_____

_____

_____

_____

_____

ASK FOR WHAT YOU REALLY WANT

Jealousy is often an indicator of desire. How can you go beyond the painful focus on what you're not getting and ask for what you want? There are many ways of asking for more of what you want. You can use assertive or dominant language and demand it (with love, of course). Or you can share your vulnerability and ask submissively for something you truly want.

For example, let's say your partner bought their new partner flowers and this made you feel jealous. You could say, "Why would you buy them flowers? You never do that for me!" Before you do, ask yourself, do you really want flowers? If so, you're more likely to get what you want by asking for it directly.

Assertive way: "I love it when you buy me flowers. Please try to do that more."

Or the more vulnerable way: "I felt jealous when you bought Andy flowers because I realized I really cherish the times that you've done that for me. Will you please try to do that more for me, too?"

Imagine a time when something triggered your jealousy. Practice writing your jealousies as desires or requests like we did in "The Art of Asking" (page 62). They can be assertive or vulnerable. Or you can try it both ways. How does this feel? How does it differ from how you've shared in the past?

_____

_____

_____

_____

_____

_____

_____

_____

_____

I've heard the term "compersion" used as the opposite of jealousy, but I can't imagine feeling happy about my partner sleeping with other people. Is compersion something I can learn?

Compersion, or the feeling of happiness or joy (rather than jealousy) when your partner romantically or sexually interacts with another person, is definitely something to strive for, and it's a skill that can be learned. But like most things, it's not a binary where compersion is on one end and jealousy is on the other. They aren't mutually exclusive. Just because you are able to feel compersion doesn't mean you'll never feel jealous. I have seen that when people feel heard and understood, it's easier to work through fears and get to what's underneath—love and joy. Sometimes people will get a tiny glimpse of compersion. With attention, that feeling can grow and can become more of a habit.

Try to practice feeling compersion by thinking of all the benefits your partner may receive from their other relationships. Then think about how these benefits will improve your own life. List them here.

_____

_____

_____

_____

_____

_____

_____

_____

_____

_____

_____

_____

_____

_____

_____

_____

_____

_____

TAKE A BREAK

When people are new to polyamory or if they just have new partners, they often spend a lot of time processing everything ad nauseum. This can be fun and exciting, but it can also distract from existing relationships or other important life events. Like any good thing, you need to have limits and practice moderation. Sometimes I suggest that people have a certain time of day that they can talk about their polyamorous relationships and other times when such discussion is off-limits. Go on a date and don't talk about any other partners. Practice going out with an existing partner or friend and *don't* talk about anyone in your polycule! How was that for you?

_____

_____

_____

_____

_____

_____

_____

_____

_____

_____

_____

_____

"SHOUTING 'SELF-CARE' AT PEOPLE WHO ACTUALLY NEED COMMUNITY CARE IS HOW WE FAIL PEOPLE."

—NAKITA VALERIO

PRACTICING
SELF-CARE

It's hard to enter into or maintain a healthy relationship if you don't feel like your best self. Despite the many popular messages of the importance of self-care, we don't heal in solitude. We are wounded in relationships, and we heal in relationships. We need community care as much as we need self-care. But it starts with you; it starts with caring for yourself with love and compassion and then extending that out to your close relationships, your local community, and the world at large. Practicing self-care—emotional, mental, and sexual—helps you bring your best, most wise and mature self to bear in all of your relationships.

Somehow, doing a face mask or taking a bath doesn't make me feel that much better when I'm overwhelmed by my issues surrounding polyamory. What do you mean by "self-care"?

Self-care goes way beyond face masks and baths, though they can be part of it. It's caring for all aspects of yourself, your body, your mind, your heart. It's a lifestyle, not a one-time act. There's a whole self-care industrial complex that is designed to profit from your desire to "treat yourself." And it's okay to engage with that from time to time. But what I'm talking about is the longer, slower, deeper, and less glamorous kind of self-care. It's about really tuning in to what you need on the deepest levels and giving it to yourself. It starts with and is maintained by having compassion and kindness for yourself in all situations. It's simple but not easy.

Let's start with the present moment. Check in with yourself right now. How do you feel so far working through this journal? What feelings has it helped you explore? What are some interesting things you have learned about yourself and your relationships?

_____

_____

_____

_____

_____

_____

_____

_____

_____

_____

_____

_____

_____

_____

_____

_____

_____

_____

_____

Imagine your perfect day of doing activities just for yourself. What would that be like?

_____

_____

_____

_____

_____

_____

_____

_____

_____

_____

_____

_____

_____

_____

_____

_____

_____

_____

_____

ENVISIONING YOUR BEST SELF

One way to get to where you want to be is to imagine you are already there. One exercise I do with my clients is having them imagine themselves as their best, most mature self and then imagine a triggering situation and play the tape forward to picture how their ideal self would respond.

- Imagine yourself as your best self. What do you feel in your body? What do you look like? What would others see and feel if they saw you in this state?

- Now imagine your partner coming home from a date with a new potential partner. How does this best version of yourself respond? Let your imagination flow!

- Take a few minutes to jot down some insights.

_____

_____

_____

_____

_____

_____

_____

_____

_____

_____

_____

Write a list of affirmations about dealing with jealousy. You can research affirmations online for inspiration or try to write your own. Start by using an "I" statement and make it in the present tense. For example, "I can handle any emotion. I'm learning to tolerate my natural feelings more and more."

_____

_____

_____

_____

_____

_____

_____

_____

_____

_____

_____

_____

_____

_____

_____

_____

_____

_____

What are the best ways you take care of yourself? In what areas of your life do you need to do better at taking care of yourself? Think of areas such as physical health, emotional health, your space/environment, work, social life, and creative pursuits.

_____

_____

_____

_____

_____

_____

_____

_____

_____

_____

_____

_____

_____

_____

_____

_____

What more do you want to do for your physical, mental, and spiritual health? Write a to-do list for each category.

_____

_____

_____

_____

_____

_____

_____

_____

_____

_____

_____

_____

_____

_____

_____

_____

_____

_____

_____

_____

LITTLE BOOK OF DESIRES

I'm like a broken record with my clients when it comes to talking about keeping a journal. It's no surprise that I'm writing this journal on exploring and navigating poly-amorous relationships! I think journaling is a powerful, lifelong tool for self-reflection. Filling out the prompts in this book is a great guided introduction to journaling, but after you're done, you can keep it going any way you want.

One technique I have found fun and illuminating is keeping a specific journal just for things I desire. Anytime I find myself daydreaming about something, I make a note in my little book of desires. They can be big or small things, realistic or not. The point is to help you become more aware of what your needs and wants are. What inspires you? What tempts you? What lights you up, and what gets you excited? Write down your answers in a separate small notebook or journal of your choosing, and keep adding to it as new ideas occur to you.

Having honest conversations about your sexual health, despite the stigma of STIs, becomes even more important when you're talking about being sexual with multiple people. When was the last time you had a checkup and STI screening? How does it feel to have these conversations with new or existing partners? How do you feel about your status?

_____

_____

_____

_____

_____

_____

_____

_____

_____

_____

_____

_____

_____

_____

_____

_____

_____

_____

DATE YOURSELF

Newly polyamorous people are often very focused on others—their current partners, new partners, or potential partners. There can also be pressure to have someone to date if one or more of your partners is dating other people. But being with yourself is an often-forgotten art. In this exercise, plan an elaborate date with yourself.

To prepare, find something to wear that makes you feel great; then go do something fun that you would want a date to do with you. Perhaps it's seeing a movie none of your partners want to see or going to a jazz bar and ordering a cocktail. Perhaps it's staying in and soaking in a bubble bath surrounded by a ton of candles. Whatever it is, woo yourself, and don't be afraid to be a little cheesy!

Take a moment now to jot down some ideas for an enjoyable night out with yourself.

How do you know when you're connected to your authentic self? When do you feel the most connected to yourself? What are you usually doing?

_____

_____

_____

_____

_____

_____

_____

_____

_____

_____

_____

_____

_____

_____

_____

_____

_____

_____

FIND YOUR GLIMMERS

When we're feeling depleted, it's hard to think of what we need to get nourished. Polyvagal theory (a theory of how our nervous system interacts with the environment to protect ourselves and connect with others) describes the concept of "glimmers" as the opposite of triggers. Glimmers help cue us back to safety and calm. On a separate sheet of paper, list all the pleasurable and/or nurturing activities you like to do, no matter how big or small. Hang the list on your refrigerator so it's visible when you need it. You could also decorate a box or a jar and write all these glimmers on small slips of paper that you put inside. Pull them out when you need them.

Often, we hold ourselves back from being who we are out of fear of disappointing others. This can stifle authenticity and creativity. Whom are you most afraid of disappointing? How can you let go of that fear?

_____

_____

_____

_____

_____

_____

_____

_____

_____

_____

_____

_____

_____

_____

_____

_____

_____

_____

_____

It's easy to fall into habitual patterns of obligation in all areas of our lives. Take some time to think about whether you do the tasks you regularly do by choice or just out of habit. For example, perhaps you find yourself dreading Sunday evenings because you have dinner with a partner's parents who don't approve of your relationship. Is it really important to you or your partner to see them this often? Perhaps your partner could go alone or the two of you could do something else on some Sundays. Think of three tasks or commitments you feel ready to let go of because they don't serve you anymore.

_____

_____

_____

_____

_____

_____

_____

_____

_____

_____

_____

_____

_____

_____

_____

_____

Tending to your physical body is an important but often neglected practice. List three ways you can be kinder to your body.

_____

_____

_____

_____

_____

_____

_____

_____

_____

_____

_____

_____

_____

_____

_____

_____

_____

Time management is a constant consideration for polyamorous people. Think of some things you can make more time for in order to nourish yourself.

Part of strengthening your connection to yourself and seeing yourself as a separate being from your romantic relationship(s) involves filling your life with things besides romance and dating. What are your hobbies, interests, and passions? What would you like to learn more about?

_____

_____

_____

_____

_____

_____

_____

_____

_____

_____

_____

_____

_____

_____

_____

_____

_____

_____

CLAIM YOUR SPACE

I really believe that our external environment can reflect our internal experience. Keeping up with household chores and maintaining a tidy space can be hard, especially if you are really busy, share space with others, or have health/mobility challenges. But cleaning and/or reorganizing even just one small part of your space can feel deeply refreshing. I often recommend focusing on the bathroom when I work with clients who feel stuck in other areas of their lives. If that's challenging for you, maybe you can enlist a friend or hire someone to help you. Once you've cleared out some space, make a self-love altar. Get a small table or shelf and put a mirror above it. Add any items that bring you joy and inspire love or beauty. You might adorn it with fresh flowers or a candle that you love the scent of. Maybe add a picture of you from when you were a child so you remember to care for all the tenderest parts of yourself.

Practice asking yourself what you need from the day rather than what the day requires of you. This can help you center yourself and strengthen your connection to self. What do you need from today? How can you remember to ask yourself this every day?

_____

_____

_____

_____

_____

_____

_____

_____

_____

_____

_____

_____

_____

_____

_____

_____

_____

_____

"WE ARE ALREADY FOUND, ALREADY TRULY, ENTIRELY, WILDLY, MESSILY, MARVELOUSLY WHO WE WERE BORN TO BE."

—ANNE LAMOTT

 How do I balance what I need and what others (partners, friends, family, community) need?

 Like everything, self-care and community care are not part of an either/or binary. It's important to do both things that are just for you and things that consider the needs of the people in your chosen community. Often, doing things that fulfill the needs of the collective is very rewarding to us as individuals. But sometimes we become too other-focused and lose ourselves. There's no perfect way to stay in balance; rather, it's important to constantly assess whether you're feeling fulfilled and connected. Some people will need more alone time, while others will need more community care. This could be protests, random acts of kindness, mutual aid in your local community, or organizing with other activists to enact social change. It can be any act of compassion. Unlike the typical picture of self-care being about rest, community care may not be as restful, but it is purposeful and may help create more meaning in your life.

A BRIEF GUIDE FOR THE LOVER(S) OF _____

Online dating profiles have helped people spell out who they are and what they want, but those have gotten shorter and shorter with the swiping technology of the latest apps. Think about going back to a longer form: writing a guide or manual for anyone who might want to be in a relationship with you. Here are some pointed questions to get you started.

- What is most important to you in your relationships?

- Do you prefer kitchen table (where all members of the polycule could sit at the table and have dinner together) or parallel (where relationships are separate and the other partners rarely interact with each other) polyam relationships?

- Do you prefer hierarchical or nonhierarchical relationships?

- How much disclosure do you like to receive from partners?

- How much time do you like to commit to relationships?

- What's your conflict style?

- How do you apologize, and how do you like to be apologized to?

- Are you a slow burn, or do you tend to burn hot and fast?

- How do you want to be informed about or introduced to potential new or existing partners of your partners (i.e., metamours)?

This can be a living, breathing document that you edit as you learn more about yourself in polyamorous relationships. You don't have to share it with anyone if you don't want to—but I suggest you do!

*Practicing gratitude has an amazing uplifting effect, and it can help you see
the world from a more positive perspective. It may sound too simple, but it's
true. Write a simple gratitude list: What are you grateful for? Maybe think of
something small you can do to celebrate some of the things on your list.*

_____

_____

_____

_____

_____

_____

_____

_____

_____

_____

_____

_____

_____

_____

_____

_____

_____

_____

_____

"LET THERE BE SPACES
IN YOUR TOGETHERNESS."
—KHALIL GIBRAN

THRIVING IN POLYAMORY

To thrive in polyamory, you must be able to ride the ebb and flow of your shifting relationships: the highs and lows, meeting new people and breaking up, handling transitions, and responding to change. In this section, you'll find tips and exercises to help you stay happy and healthy in your polyamorous relationships. This section might feel like it's geared toward people who are already practicing polyamory, but the insights can be useful whether you're in a monogamous or a polyamorous relationship.

Think of three relationship dreams related to polyamory that you would like to manifest this year. Focus on the feeling, not the form (e.g., "I dream of feeling showered in love and support so that my heart feels so full" rather than, "I want one partner who likes to do this and one who likes to do that.").

Think of a time you felt very loved and cared for by someone. What was that like? What did they do to make you feel loved?

_____

_____

_____

_____

_____

_____

_____

_____

_____

_____

_____

_____

_____

_____

_____

_____

_____

_____

Write your future love story. Let yourself dream big. Write it as if it's already happening. How many partners do you have? What roles does each one play in your life? What does your living situation look like? What is your life like?

An unexpected challenge people practicing ethical non-monogamy may encounter is feeling like they don't deserve all the love they're receiving by having multiple partners. Do you feel capable of accepting and giving love to multiple people? How can you open yourself up to more love?

Breaking up is a skill that our mononormative culture doesn't adequately teach us. I think that's part of why breakups are so painful and disorienting. The fact is that most people are going to have at least one breakup and probably many more, especially if they're practicing polyamory. (Just based on numbers, the more people you date, the more likely you are to experience a breakup.) Like dealing with jealousy, respectfully breaking up is another skill that must be developed. How do you normally handle breakups? How, if at all, would you like to handle them differently?

_____

_____

_____

_____

_____

_____

_____

_____

_____

_____

_____

_____

_____

_____

_____

RADAR CHECK-IN

I recommend that my clients do a regular check-in meeting with each person they're in a dyad (two-person relationship) with, in addition to their therapy sessions with me. One check-in activity I recommend is from the podcast *Multiamory*; it's called RADAR, which stands for review, agree, discuss, action points, reconnect. Using the below format for structuring your check-ins helps ensure that everyone gets their needs addressed. I recommend coming prepared as if it were a work meeting and taking notes. Relationships, after all, take work!

Review what's happened since the last RADAR check-in. It can be helpful to look back at the notes you took last time. Celebrate which actions points you did successfully! If there are any you didn't complete, put them back on the agenda.

Agree on an agenda. Make sure you've added everything you want to discuss; then decide on the order of topics. Some ideas for topics include quality time, sex, health, other partners, fights/arguments, money, work/projects, travel, family (kids, relatives, parents), and household issues.

Discuss the items on your agenda, and talk openly. Try to get to all of the topics, even if everything is okay in that area and it doesn't require a lot of discussion.

Action points are achievable goals that are as specific as possible. Who is in charge of what, what will happen, and when will it happen?

Reconnect to share appreciation. Take turns sharing and listening. Give each other compliments. Do a fun activity, like a massage or cuddle, or have sex.

Polyamory allows for a supportive network of relationships that share resources and absorb the stresses of modern life in a different way than a monogamous nuclear family can. How does your interest in polyamory inform your definitions of family? Does this affect how you share resources or how you want to?

_____

_____

_____

_____

_____

_____

_____

_____

_____

_____

_____

_____

_____

_____

_____

_____

_____

_____

_____

My partner seems to keep dating people who are interested in a monogamous relationship, and these relationships often end when they see that I'm not going away. This seems to cause heartache for everyone involved. Can mono/polyam relationships ever work?

Mono/polyam relationships *can* work. I've seen it happen. But I will say, it requires a lot of effort. No matter what the relationship structure is, each person needs to decide for themselves what their relationship orientation is. Monogamy can be part of your identity, but if your partner is non-monogamous and actively partnering with others, you are likely going to be in a non-monogamous relationship. As for repeatedly dating monogamous people, this is a pretty common occurrence. The dating pool is limited for polyamorous people, so when you meet someone who is at least open to dating, even if deep down they want monogamy, it's hard not to pursue that person. Sometimes polyamory sounds nice in theory, but people find out it's not for them in practice. But more often, people don't know that they strongly prefer monogamy until they try the other side. My advice is to stay open and try to allow people to be dynamic as they explore their identities.

"EACH FRIEND REPRESENTS A WORLD IN US, A WORLD POSSIBLY NOT BORN UNTIL THEY ARRIVE, AND IT IS ONLY BY THIS MEETING THAT A NEW WORLD IS BORN."

—ANAÏS NIN

What are the best ways to come out to our family and friends?

As you may have noticed by now, I don't believe there's one best way to do anything. As far as coming out, there are many different ways to do it. Some people gather their loved ones together and make a big announcement. Others start bringing other partners to family gatherings and let their families make whatever assumptions they may. Others share their polyamorous identity and relationships loud and proud on social media. It's up to you and everyone involved. Sometimes one partner wants to be out while the other does not, so you have to negotiate what feels good for everyone. Often children can tell something is going on and have an easy time understanding that their parents have multiple lovers. Speak to them at their level of understanding and reassure them that they are loved.

Coming out is a big consideration. Some non-monogamous people are also LGBTQIA2S+, and so they may have some experience with coming out already (although not necessarily). Still, there are many polyamorous people who have never experienced the stigma of being marginalized—and all the feelings that go along with that. What is your experience with coming out? If you're not out, do you want to be? To whom and how would you like to come out?

New relationship energy (NRE) is something polyamorous people are always talking about. It describes the exciting rush of emotions that come when you first start dating someone. It's often discussed as something to be wary of because people can act in irrational ways when they are newly falling in love. Have you ever experienced NRE? How do you manage it?

_____

_____

_____

_____

_____

_____

_____

_____

_____

_____

_____

_____

_____

_____

_____

_____

_____

DRAW YOUR POLYCULE

Now let's have some fun and draw your polycule. Besides a good excuse to get out those markers or colored pencils, drawing your polycule can help you understand how many people are in your orbit and remember who is on the minds of you and your partners. (Recall that a polycule is all of your partners and all of their partners and their partners.) I've included a simple example below. You can be as detailed as you want; no artistic ability is needed!

On a separate sheet of paper, just start with a circle with your name and then draw lines to each of the people in your polycule. They can be lovers, platonic life partners, crushes, anchor partners (kind of like nesting partners but not necessarily someone you live with), and any other auxiliary partners. If you are artistically inclined, make it beautiful and hang it on your refrigerator or frame it as a gift. Or try contacting the artist Tikva Wolf of Kimchi Cuddles (see the Recommended Resources, page 156) who will draw a portrait for you and your polycule if you send in pictures.

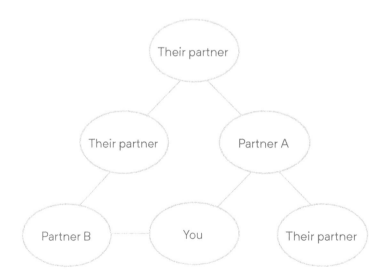

"Polysaturation" is a term polyamorous people use to describe when they are at maximum capacity for partners. What does polysaturation look or feel like for you? What are the signs that you might be stretched too thin?

_____

_____

_____

_____

_____

_____

_____

_____

_____

_____

_____

_____

_____

_____

_____

_____

_____

_____

_____

Established relationship energy (ERE), as opposed to NRE, describes all the feelings and emotions that come from being in established relationships. For example, maybe it's a sense of calm, the ease of communication, or the comfortable predictability of routines. It's a totally different energy and often something that polyamorous people appreciate having in addition to NRE. What are all the things you appreciate about ERE? What do you love about being in established relationships? Have you shared this with the people with whom you are in established relationships?

DATE JAR

Deciding what to eat for dinner or what to do for dates doesn't get any easier when you have more partners. Think of dates or things you would like to do by yourself or with your partner(s), write them on slips of paper, and put them in a jar. Use one color of paper for things you want to do by yourself and different colors for things you want to do with different partners. Don't be afraid to ask your lovers or friends for ideas! When your jar is full, share it with whomever you want to go on the dates with. Maybe if you have a set day and time, you or your partner(s) can pull an idea out and then go with that date for that night.

I feel like my mental health is declining because of all the added stress of polyamory. What if my trauma history will make it too hard to be in a polyamorous relationship?

It's not always the right time to be practicing polyamory. I have seen people in various stages of recovery from trauma try to open their relationships, only to be overwhelmed and retraumatized. It doesn't mean they can't do it—just that they may need to go slowly, they may need additional reassurances, or they may need to do some more work in therapy before moving forward. Make sure you have a good trauma-informed therapist who is polyamory friendly as well. Check out the Recommended Resources section (page 156) for directories to find practitioners. Many times, what is coming up is offering an opportunity to be healed, but you need the right supports and environment to do that.

Practicing polyamory can be a wild ride. The rush of meeting a new person you connect with can be exhilarating. The pain of rejection by someone you were really excited about can hurt as well, even though you still have other relationships. The fear you feel when your partner goes on a new date, even after you're riding high from your own date the previous night, can feel disorienting. How can you try to have mental calmness as you go through the highs and lows of polyamory? How can you keep your feet steady on the ground?

CREATE A RECONNECTION RITUAL

When your partner returns from a date, there can be a wide range of feelings and reactions. Some people find themselves wanting to hear about everything, some need some reassurance that their partner is glad to be home, and some don't want to talk at all until they've had a good night's sleep. Everyone needs different rituals to reconnect after their partner has had a date with someone else. Let's figure out what works for you.

Imagine your partner has come home from a date with a partner they are really excited about. What is your immediate reaction? Do you wish this reaction was different? If so, how?

_____

_____

_____

What would help you feel connected again? Some examples might be going out and talking in a neutral space (about the date or anything else), having sex and communicating through touch how much you missed each other, or showering together and washing each other.

_____

_____

_____

Now, try making a clear request for something that will help you feel connected to your partner and your relationship, and then do it. You might need to try something else after the next date before you find a ritual that usually works.

Sometimes people are so wrapped up in their own polycule dynamics that they forget to turn their attention outward and get advice or inspiration from people outside their romantic/sexual relationships. Make a list of the people outside your polycule whom you can rely on for support when you need it. They may or may not be polyamorous; they just need to be people who support your choices.

CONNECT WITH COMMUNITY

Being connected to a community of people who are practicing or have had experience with polyamory is key to getting the support you need to make polyamorous relationships work. Learning about the struggles other people are going through can be so validating and can remind you that you aren't the only person facing challenges in this lifestyle. It's also a great way to learn about a variety of different relationship structures, as well as tips and tricks on how to make them work.

To learn more about what types of people you would like to be in community with, make a list of all the inspiring polyamorous relationships you know of, even if you only know them through social media, TV, or movies. What do you like about them? Are there aspects of these relationships you aspire toward?

_____

_____

_____

_____

_____

_____

Now get started on seeking out community. Are there any polyamorous discussion circles or meetup groups in your area? Would you consider attending a polyamorous conference? Research what's out there and make a list of the opportunities that pique your interest. (Check the Recommended Resources, page 156, for a start.)

_____

_____

_____

_____

PLAN A METAMOUR HANGOUT

One of the best pieces of advice I ever got when I was first starting out in polyamory was to meet your metamours. Metamours are your partners' other partners, and they are the glue that hold polycules together. It may sound scary—and it is!—but in my experience (and in the experience of many other people I've worked with), meeting the other person(s) reduces jealousy. You see that they are human just like you, and when you have a direct connection with them, they tend to be more considerate of you and your needs. This doesn't mean you have to practice kitchen table polyamory, but I think at least meeting once will go a long way.

Think of a metamour you either haven't met or haven't gotten to connect with as much as you'd like. What could you do with them? Go vintage shopping? Try a new restaurant your partner isn't interested in? Look for a birthday gift for your shared partner?

Reach out to them and say something genuine and affirming. Share if you're nervous or if you feel brave.

If and when you go hang out with them, share what that was like. Was it what you expected? Did you feel differently about them by the end of your time together? Did you feel differently about them dating your partner? What kind of relationship would you like with them moving forward?

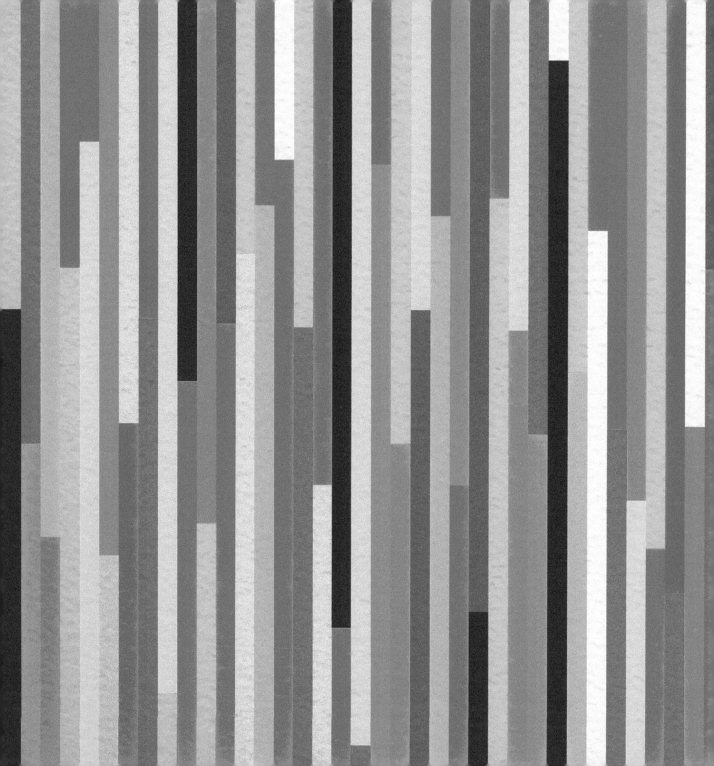

A FINAL WORD

I hope this journal has helped you learn something new about yourself, your relationships, and what you need to feel loved, supported, and nurtured. I hope it helps you keep getting to know yourself, be brave enough to admit what you desire, and be courageous enough to share it with the people in your life. When you're authentic about who you are and what you need, it demonstrates trust. Be patient with yourself; this is a lifelong journey. And don't be surprised that, if you work through this journal again in five years, you might answer some things very differently.

Every relationship is unique, and if you allow them to be, they can change you in ways you never imagined—hopefully for the better. I believe every person you're intimately connected with is like a mirror and has something to show you about yourself.

Healing is about remembering the wisdom that you already have. Keep this journal as a way to remember who you are (at least in this time and place when you did the work of completing it) and what you need. Let your own words be a soothing balm if you're struggling with some aspect of polyamory in the future. Let these discoveries guide you and remind you and the people you're in relationships with of what you need to be happy and fulfilled. Return to it regularly, if that feels good, and keep it going with your own ideas and prompts. Feel free to reach out to your friends, your partners, your polycule, and your community. Remember, you have within and around you all the answers you need!

RECOMMENDED RESOURCES

Books

***Building Open Relationships: Your Hands-On Guide to Swinging, Polyamory, and Beyond!* by Dr. Liz Powell (Dr. Liz Powell, 2018)**
Many people in my polyam community recommend this book for newbies looking to venture into opening their relationship.

***Love's Not Colorblind: Race and Representation in Polyamorous and Other Alternative Communities* by Kevin Patterson (Thorntree Press, 2018)**
An important take on race and representation in queer and polyamorous communities.

***Opening Up: A Guide to Creating and Sustaining Open Relationships* by Tristan Taormino (Cleis Press, 2008)**
This book was my guide when I was first being openly ethically non-monogamous many years ago.

***Pleasure Activism: The Politics of Feeling Good* by adrienne maree brown (AK Press, 2019)**
A soothing balm and powerful manifesto that will help you feel empowered to do what makes you happy and what is pleasurable.

***Polysecure: Attachment, Trauma, and Consensual Nonmonogamy* by Jessica Fern (Thorntree Press, 2020)**
A book written by a polyamorous therapist explaining attachment theory and how to apply it to ethically non-monogamous relationship structures.

Websites

Kimchi Cuddles
KimchiCuddles.com
The website of artist Tikva Wolf, it includes her comics focusing on communication effectiveness and relationship dynamics.

Kink-Aware Professionals
KAPprofessionals.org
This is a list of professionals (therapists, doctors, and others) who are non-monogamy and kink aware and affirming.

Poly-Friendly Professionals
PolyFriendly.org
Use this list to find therapists who self-identify as non-monogamy affirming.

Relationship Anarchy Manifesto
**TheAnarchistLibrary.org/library/andie-nordgren-the-short-instructional
-manifesto-for-relationship-anarchy**
A short instructional manifesto for relationship anarchy, a philosophy that falls under the umbrella of ethical non-monogamy.

Scarleteen
Scarleteen.com
A robust resource on sexuality and relationships. It's geared to teens, but I find the easy-to-read and progressive articles to be helpful for adults, too.

Podcasts

Making Polyamory Work
Podcasts.apple.com/us/podcast/making-polyamory-work/id1487987837
Hosted by a queer, non-monogamous mom, this podcast tackles all the topics needed to make polyamory work.

Multiamory
Multiamory.com/podcast
A lively and fun podcast hosted by three people who used to be in a triad.

Poly Weekly
PolyWeekly.com
This podcast has been running for years, so it has a ton of veteran advice for people of all levels of experience with ethical non-monogamy.

Polycurious
Podcasts.apple.com/us/podcast/polycurious/id1558602197
A podcast hosted by a young femme person who is navigating a mono/polyam relationship and having thoughtful conversations on important polyamory topics.

Instagram Accounts

@bygabriellesmith
Intersectional polyamory educator sharing lots of important polyamory information in easy-to-read, succinct graphics.

@chillpolyamory
Queer polyamory mentor who provides a lot of helpful definitions and quippy reels.

@lavitaloca34
Personal coach specializing in relationship dynamics and non-monogamy.

@marjanilane
Pro-Black polyam education with cool, thought-provoking graphics.

@remodeledlove
Polyamorous mama expanding the cultural narrative on healthy relationships.

Conferences and Organizations

Loving More
LovingMoreNonprofit.org
A conference in Denver and Philadelphia and one of the first ethical non-monogamy conferences in the United States.

The Network/La Red
TNLR.org
Survivor-led organization working to end partner abuse in LGBTQ+, SM, and polyamorous communities.

Sex Down South
SexDownSouth.com
An annual conference in Atlanta with a focus on QTBIPOC sex and non-monogamy educators.

Southwest Love Fest
SWLoveFest.com
An annual conference in Tucson that I cocreated that explores relationships, identity, ethical non-monogamy, and community. Very sex-positive, fun, and thoughtful. Think academic conference meets Burning Man.

Tucson Counseling Associates
TucsonCounselingAssociates.com
Anti-oppressive mental health clinic specializing in working with LGBTQIA2S+ and ethically non-monogamous people. This is the practice I founded in 2015.

REFERENCES

Chapais, Bernard. "Monogamy, Strongly Bonded Groups, and the Evolution of Human Social Structure." *Evolutionary Anthropology* 22, no. 2 (March–April 2013): 52–65. DOI.org/10.1002/evan.21345.

Dana, Deb. *Polyvagal Exercises for Safety and Connection.* New York: W. W. Norton and Company, 2020.

Fern, Jessica. *Polysecure: Attachment, Trauma, and Consensual Nonmonogamy.* Portland: Thorntree Press, 2020.

Hardy, Janet, and Dossie Easton. *The Ethical Slut: A Practical Guide to Polyamory, Open Relationships & Other Adventures.* Berkeley: Ten Speed Press, 2017.

Harris, Russ. *The Happiness Trap: How to Stop Struggling and Start Living.* Boston: Trumpeter Books, 2008.

Hayes, Steven C., and Spencer Smith. *Get Out of Your Mind and Into Your Life: The New Acceptance and Commitment Therapy.* Oakland: New Harbinger Publications, 2005.

Labriola, Kathy. *The Jealousy Workbook: Exercises and Insights for Managing Open Relationships.* Emeryville: Greenery Press, 2013.

Moors, Amy, Amanda Gesselman, and Justin Garcia. "Desire, Familiarity, and Engagement in Polyamory: Results from a National Sample of Single Adults in the United States." *Frontiers in Psychology* 12 (March 2021). DOI.org/10.3389/fpsyg.2021.619640.

Multiamory. "R.A.D.A.R." Accessed October 11, 2021. Multiamory.com/radar.

Rosenberg, Marshall. *Nonviolent Communication: A Language of Compassion.* Encinitas: PuddleDancer Press, 1999.

Ryan, Christopher, and Jetha Cacilda. *Sex at Dawn: The Prehistoric Origins of Modern Sexuality*. New York: Harper, 2010.

Savage, Dan. "Podcast #66: Dan Savage on Monogamy." Savage Lovecast. June 23, 2015. Savage.love/lovecast.

Urbaniak, Kasia. *Unbound: A Woman's Guide to Power*. New York: Tarcherperigee, 2020.

Van Anders, Sari. "Beyond Sexual Orientation: Integrating Gender/Sex and Diverse Sexualities via Sexual Configurations Theory." *Archives of Sexual Behavior* 44, no. 5 (July 2015): 1177–1213. DOI.org/10.1007/s10508-015-0490-8.

Wismeiher, Andreas, and Marcel A. L. M van Assen. "Psychological Characteristics of BDSM Practitioners." *The Journal of Sexual Medicine* 10, no. 8 (May 2013): 1943–1952. DOI.org/10.1111/jsm.12192.

ACKNOWLEDGMENTS

To my anchor partner, Joseph; thank you for watching our cute baby and adjusting your life and schedule to support my big dreams. Thank you also for challenging me and reflecting the ways I can't see myself. Thank you to my son, Roscoe, and all of my descendants for making me long for life and inspiring me to build something new and better for our future. Thank you to all of my past partners who were with me in the early, scary days of my exploration of ethical non-monogamy. And thank you to all of my metamours, some of whom are still dear friends. You taught me some of the most valuable lessons about life and love. Thank you to my cocreators of Southwest Love Fest and all the people in Love Is Not a Finite Resource. These two passion projects helped support me in many unseen ways as I explored my own polyamorous identity. Lastly, thank you to all of my clients who are bravely exploring polyamory and allowing me to witness and support you in the process.

ABOUT THE AUTHOR

 Kate Kincaid, LPC, is a licensed professional counselor in Tucson, Arizona. She founded and runs a group private practice that specializes in working with LGBTQIA2S+ clients, people in ethically non-monogamous relationships, perinatal mental health, and psychedelic-assisted psychotherapy. She is also the cocreator of Southwest Love Fest, a conference on relationships, identity, and community. Kate's therapeutic style is informed by feminism and social justice, seeking to help collectively dismantle systems of violence and oppression. She believes that many issues people come to therapy with are rooted in a logical response to an oppressive system, which is then pathologized and stigmatized. In her free time, she likes to chase around her toddler, write, make spaces more beautiful, and build communities and futures where we're all a little more safe and free.